To:

From:

To our beloved Angelia and Willie.— Sylvia Browne
and Chris Dufresne
Special thanks to Linda Rossi.

Text copyright © 2007 Sylvia Browne and Chris Dufresne
Edited by Kat Shehata
Design by Jo McElwee
Images copyright © 2007 Shutterstock
First U.S. edition 2007
Printed in China

Bibliography for "True Stories"
"Animals Sensed Tsunami?" Reuters. 30 Dec. 2004. www.aljazeera.net.
"Lions Free Kidnapped Girl." CNN. 22 June 2005 www.nazret.com.
"Lions Free Kidnapped Girl." 21 June 2005 www.all-creatures.org.
Ngow, Rodrique. "Kenya: Stray Dog Saves Abandoned Baby."
Associated Press. 10 May 2005 www.espn.go.com.
"Police: Lions Free Kidnapped Girl." Associated Press. 21 June 2005
www.nazret.com.
Reagan, Ron. "Man's Best Friend." MSNBC. 13 May 2005
www.msnbc.msn.com.
"Saved by a Sixth Sense." 04 Jan. 2005 www.beliefnet.com.
"Stray Dog Saves Baby." Permalink. 10 May 2005 www.sushiesque.com.
"Tsunami: Animal Instinct." Animal Planet. 08 Aug. 2005
www.animalplanet.co.uk.

Browne, Sylvia.
         Spirit of Animals / by Sylvia Browne and Chris
         Dufresne.
            p. cm.
         ISBN 0-9777790-1-7

         1. Guides (Spiritualism) 2. Animals--Miscellanea.
         3. Human-animal communication. 4. Future life.
         I. Dufresne, Chris. II. Title.
         BF1275.G85B77 2007   133'.259
                        QBI06-600385

Angel Bea Publishing
www.angelbea.com

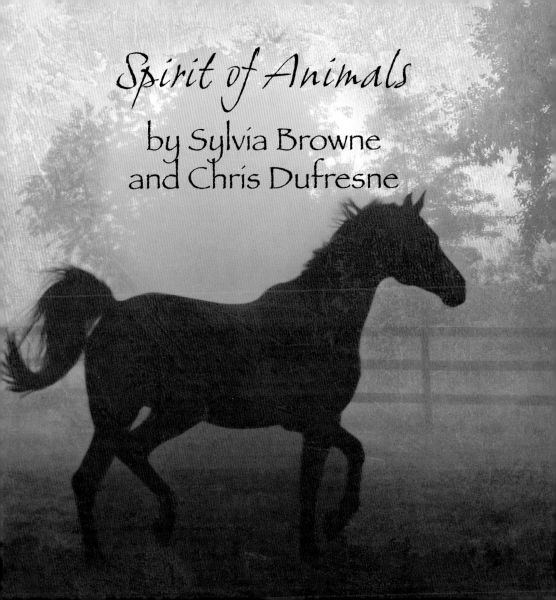

Spirit of Animals

by Sylvia Browne
and Chris Dufresne

*F*or most of us, in this lifetime or any other, the most difficult moments of our lives stem from the loss of a family member. If you are an animal lover like me, the loss of a beloved pet is as devastating as the loss of a person. Let me tell you, without a shadow of doubt, our pets will be waiting for us on the Other Side.

—Sylvia Browne

*A*ll the pets I have had throughout
my life are still with me to this day.

*The spirit of my dog, Lance,
is always with our family.*

Although he died many years ago,
he is still around playing and
watching over us the way he
always did. All of our other pets
see him, too, and play with him
just as if he never left.
—Chris Dufresne

$\mathcal{A}$nimals do not come into the world
to learn and experience life like we do.

They are perfect just
the way
God made them.

It is no mystery to animals that they
will live for all eternity. In fact, it is for
this reason that there are no animal
ghosts. —Sylvia Browne

$\mathcal{O}$n the Other Side we chart out our lives before we incarnate. We choose a life theme, who we will marry, how many children we will have, and where we will live.

We even choose our pets.

We do this so that we can elevate our spirits and learn from these particular experiences. To help us stay on track with our goals, we choose a spirit guide to accompany us while we are away from Home. For protection on our journey, we also choose a certain number of angels to watch over us, as well as an animal spirit, called a totem. —Chris Dufresne

A totem is an animal spirit, or anima, that we entrust to stand by our side throughout our lifetime. All members of the animal kingdom, from lions to peacocks, have attributes that our spirits can emulate and connect with our life theme. For example, my totem is a grizzly bear, a symbol of strength, and my life theme is "warrior." —Chris Dufresne

Some people may never actually see their totems, but the energy of their spirits is always present. My totem is an elephant: symbolic of strength and loyalty.

"What does a totem actually do for me?"

Totems serve several purposes in our lives. First of all, they serve as sentinels standing guard on our behalf. This means when totems sense dark spirits or feel we are somehow being threatened, they will instinctively try to scare off our enemies by growling, hissing, or by acting aggressively. Secondly, our totems offer us positive energy simply from their mere presence. —Sylvia Browne

Lions

Lions are recognized around the
world as symbols of strength
and majestic pride. In fact, the
lion is the totem of the most
powerful phylum of angels,
the Principalities, which are
Father God's army of angels.
—Sylvia Browne

Animals are God's perfect creations.

When our spirits are next to these wonderful creatures, their energy reflects upon our spirits. We actually feel courageous when the spirit of a lion is near us, or strong when an elephant is in our presence. Just like when you are around a person you admire or respect, you can feel the positive energy from that person. Every phylum of angels has totems, too, and these angels can call upon animals to intercede on your behalf when you need help or protection.
—Sylvia Browne

In a small village in Ethiopia, a young girl was kidnapped by a gang of men who planned to force her into marriage. For seven horrible days, the kidnappers held her captive. Her family and the police desperately searched for her,

Heaven Sent

but they were not able to track her down. The rescuers were running out of time to save the girl - until...

unlikely heroes

came to the rescue. A pride of Ethiopian lions approached the camp where the kidnappers were holding the girl. The lions encircled the victim creating a ring of protection. The mere presence of the beasts scared off the men. The plot was foiled. The lions stayed with the girl protecting her for half a day until help finally arrived. When the girl was safe, the lions left her side and went back into the forest as if their work was done.

—True story

Dearest God,
Let my spirit emulate the nature of animals.

May I always be:

grateful

for my life
and for the
opportunities
and challenges
I face in
this world,

loyal

to my
loved
ones
and to
those who
count
on me for
support,

committed

to follow
my chosen path,
no matter what
obstacles stand
before me,

have

faith

in You even
though it may
seem the world
is against me,

remain

open minded

when making
new friends,

and may I never
back down
from a

challenge,

after all, what doesn't kill us
makes us *stronger.*

—Sylvia Browne

*O*ur pets provide
unconditional love and
support throughout our
lives. Animals are natural

"negativity absorbers."

When you feel sad or
depressed, hold your
pet and feel the warmth
of its spirit. The positive
energy and love you
feel from your pet will
reflect on you and
help lift your spirit.
—Chris Dufresne

What are you so happy about?

Animals are very spiritual creatures.

They come into this world remembering life on the Other Side and knowing that life is eternal. In fact, they go Home in their sleep much more often than we do. On average, you and I astral trip about twice a week. (An astral trip is when our spirits visit the Other Side while we are sleeping.) Animals on the other hand astral trip several times a day. No wonder they like to sleep so much!
—Chris Dufresne

Falcon

A symbol of
loyalty and
perseverance

anima of Powers

Dear Chris,

I have always felt a strong connection to animals, especially dogs. The first dog I ever had was a German shepherd named Jill. One day Jill and I were playing in the backyard. For some reason, I asked her to show me where to dig to find a treasure. I held on to her collar and we walked around a bit, then she found a shady spot and laid down. "This must be the spot," I thought. "This is where the buried treasure is hidden!" Sure enough, with the naivete of a four-year-old, I began to dig in that spot with my bare hands. Believe it or not, I did unearth a couple of old coins. I don't remember how much money was there, but my dog Jill did manage to show me the money.

"Do animals have a sixth sense?"

—Letter from a reader

Show Me the Money

A true story.

*Animals do have
a sixth sense.*
Have you ever seen a dog
barking at what you
think is nothing? Think again.
They probably see something
or someone you don't.
Animals can see the spirits
of our loved ones, angels,
and spirit guides.
—Chris Dufresne

Blue light
special

A true story.

Dear Sylvia,

Growing up, we always had a houseful of dogs. I don't remember going to pick them out though; it seemed they had a way of "finding" our house. I had one dog in particular that made a lasting impression on me. One day I came home from school and a group of neighborhood kids were teasing and throwing rocks at this poor, shabby dog. I couldn't stand the sight of this so I called the dog to me to get her away from the boys. Well, she took one look at me and came running. I think she made up her mind I was the girl for her. She followed me all the way home and when I opened the front door, I think she expected to just come on in. We already had two dogs in our family. Adding another one would be a hard sell to my dad.

This dog was a mess. She had long matted hair and was filthy dirty. Her head was too big for her body and she had a big bald spot on her head from a previous injury. My dad glanced out the window at the poor dog. I could see he had sympathy for her, but he gave me a flat out, "No." I was scared the boys might hurt her again but I felt like there was nothing I could do. Before I went to bed, I peeked out my window to see if the dog had left, but I couldn't see through the darkness. After everyone went to bed for the night, we awakened to an agonizing sound. The stray dog was howling pitifully on the front lawn. My dad went outside to see what was wrong with her. I guess he thought she was in terrible pain. She did appear to be suffering. My dad patted her on the head and started talking sweetly to try to get her to stop. Since she wasn't hurt, it was apparent to me she was

pleading her case.

This dog may have been scraggly and a bit on the ugly side, but what she lacked in looks, she made up for in personality. The stray dog, we later named Sara, got her wish. We opened the front door and let her in for good.

—Letter from a reader

People have said to me over the years
"Whenever there is a stray or needy
animal in the neighborhood, they
always come to my house."

Animals, like the stray dog in the previous story, see a blue light around people who are kind to animals. Think about your own pets. Have you noticed how they react differently to certain people? Your dog may love your next door neighbor who has a houseful of cats and it may shy away or be afraid of a visitor who is not a big fan of animals. —Sylvia Browne

Every living thing has spiritual energy, or an aura, around them. As humans, we can sense each other's aura, but we do not actually see this light that encompasses our spirit. Animals, on the other hand, do see our aura.

For this reason, animals can be described as having a highly developed sixth sense.

—Chris Dufresne

Sixth Sense

Elephants are the anima of Mother God's army of angels-the Thrones.

Elephants are a common sight in Thailand. They are working animals that serve many purposes for the people of their native land. They are essential to the economy because of their marvelous appeal to tourists. On December 26th, 2004 it was business as usual on one tourist filled beach. Elephants were working giving rides and people were splashing in the waves. It seemed to be just an ordinary day. Suddenly, without cause, the elephants became agitated, extremely alert, and were not responding to their handler's commands. One elephant had a family of tourists on its back. This elephant, along with all the other elephants on the beach, inexplicably took off for higher ground despite the handler's pleas to stop. Some elephants even broke their leg chains to flee the scene.

Moments later, the Indian Ocean lifted walls of waves as high as skyscrapers and crashed them down. Thousands upon thousands of lives were lost. However, people on the scene began to notice that there didn't appear to be any animal victims. There were no dead fish, birds, dogs, cats, elephants or signs that any animals had perished. Miles away, a wave of floodwater washed through the biggest wildlife reserve in Sri Lanka. Even there, all the animals in the park avoided the path of destruction. In the eerie calm after this massive tsunami, the elephants that escaped the crushing waves on the Thai beach resurfaced. Elephants picked up survivors and put them on their backs. Some even lifted up lifeless bodies with their trunks and took them to land. In the weeks and months following the devastation, elephants were instrumental in the clean-up and restoration process. Handlers gave commands for the elephants to pick up debris from up-rooted trees and to move heavy remnants of destroyed homes with their strong trunks. The elephants worked together with workers by carrying much needed supplies like blankets, clothes, and food to survivors and rescue workers.

Elephants have always been a symbol of strength to the people of Thailand. Now, there is no question why they are so revered in their native land. —True story

Wolf

Swift messenger,

anima of Archangels

"Will I be reunited with my pets on the Other Side?"

The answer is, of course, "Yes." Trust your instincts and have faith in God. Look into your pet's eyes. It is inconceivable to think that God doesn't love this animal as much as you do. Mother God and Father God love every living thing. That is why Heaven looks just like earth in its most perfect and natural form.

—Sylvia Browne

Sylvia's Story

My dog, Jolie, and I had a very special connection. I love all my pets, but Jolie and I shared a deep bond.

Jolie lived a wonderful life. When it was time for her to go Home, I held her in my arms and rocked her as her life was coming to an end. Just as she took her last breath, I closed my eyes and saw the most magnificent sight. It was the tunnel that leads to the Other Side.

A white swirl came out of Jolie's body and a tunnel formed before her.

The white swirl took shape and I recognized it was Jolie's spirit. That little white dog I loved so much was running through the tunnel that leads to eternal happiness. I kept my eyes closed and I saw her running through a beautiful field. She was no longer in pain. She was happy. She was surrounded by the White Light of pure love that fills the spirit of every living thing. I can honestly say I was devastated by Jolie's death; of course I missed her and wanted her with me forever. However, I am very grateful for the miracle I witnessed.

—Sylvia Browne

RAVEN

Symbol of protection against dark entities,

anima of Carrion Angels

Double Take

A true story.

Dear Chris,

One day I went to
the local animal shelter
with my husband and kids
to scout out a new puppy for
our family. After meeting a couple of
prospective pets, our hearts went out to a
golden retriever mix. One look into his sweet
brown eyes and it was unanimous. He was
our new baby. I then called my mom, who
lived nearby, to come and meet our new
family member.

While the kids were playing with the puppy, my husband and I noticed an older collie in the next cage. We considered taking both of them but knew we couldn't. When my mom arrived she made her way down the hallway, past the cages, to where we were standing. Without knowing anything about our second choice dog, she glanced at the collie, stopped dead in her tracks, did a double take and said "I'm taking this one." It seemed both dogs were destined to be in our family.

"Was it a coincidence that all of us felt a connection to the collie?"

—Letter from a reader

$\mathcal{W}$hen it is written in your chart that you will
have a specific pet, trust me, your guides will
make sure you find one another.

Whether you go to the pound to pick your pet or
your pet comes to you out of the blue, you will
find a way to be together. —Chris Dufresne

SEAGULL

Symbol of

Purity,

anima of Angels

All the animals your spirit has loved throughout eternity will be with you on the Other Side.

In every life we choose we take on a different life theme. We live in a new environment in a new body. We follow a complex and highly detailed chart with a unique set of circumstances. In one life, you might have lived in Egypt and owned a camel as a pet, or you could have lived in Alaska and had a team of sled dogs.

—Chris Dufresne

All the spirits of animals, people, and nature exist in harmony on the Other Side.
Animals and people no longer have earthly instincts to "kill or be killed," and there is no need to fight over territories, property, borders, or mates since all of our needs are inherently met. Animals and people do not fear each other, rather we all live with mutual respect for one another. I am often asked if we can communicate with animals, both here and on the Other Side. I am happy to say that the answer is "yes."
—Sylvia Browne

On earth animals understand what we say when we talk to them, but they do not communicate with us by using words. Of course, they do talk to us by barking, growling, hissing, purring, braying, howling, and so on. But on the Other Side, we can communicate with animals telepathically. At Home when we want to communicate with our pets or animals, we simply need to think what we want them to know, and they will respond in kind. This is how animals communicate with one another as well.

—Chris Dufresne

Cougar

Symbol of strength and dignity,

anima of Dominions

Animal Instincts

In a small village in Nairobi, Kenya, a stray dog gave birth to a litter of puppies behind an old wooden building. The mother dog cared for her young, but she had to leave them each day to find food for herself. One day the dog ducked under a barbed-wire fence that surrounded a building and crossed the street to forage in the woods. While she was searching for a meal, she

discovered a human baby. Two children saw the mother dog carrying the baby. The children ran to their mother for help. She immediately went to check out their story. The children were correct. The woman found the dog with the puppies and the newborn baby she had apparently added to her litter.

*H*appily, the infant was taken to the hospital and received medical care. The mother dog's act of heroism was rewarded by the community. She is now named Saviour and will never go hungry again.   —True story

CANARY

Spreading joy
through
music,

anima of Cherubim
and Seraphim angels

People often wonder how we are able to find all of our pets and loved ones on the Other Side.

Don't worry, our loved ones know when we are coming Home. Each spirit has a light. When our souls are ready to make the transition to the Other Side, each light flashes to inform loved ones we are on the way. At any time, spirits on the Other Side can check in on us to see how we are doing. Like watching a television show, they can see us whenever they choose.

—Sylvia Browne

On the Other Side,
animals typically reside in
the same environment
they thrived in on earth.

Although they may roam wherever
they choose, you will typically see
polar bears in Alaska, sea lions
in California, giraffes in Africa,
and so on. —Chris Dufresne

Do our pets miss us?

The answer which may alarm some of you is, "No." Animals have a divine sense of the afterlife. They are infused with the knowledge that life is forever and "goodbye" is only temporary. When our spirits come to earth, we have what I describe as "amnesia." In order to perfect our souls by experiencing negativity, we must forget our perfect lives waiting for us on the Other Side, or at least tuck them away in our subconscious for awhile. That is not to say that we don't have faith in God and the afterlife, but we have to be infused with a sense of wonder. If we could all recall how great we have it on the Other Side, everyone would check out of here without fulfilling their goals.

—Chris Dufresne

Living Angels

About the Authors

Sylvia Browne

Millions of people have witnessed Sylvia Browne's incredible psychic powers on TV shows such as *Montel*, *Larry King Live*, *Entertainment Tonight*, and *Unsolved Mysteries*. Sylvia is the author of numerous books and audios, and has recently launched her own merchandise line, The Sylvia Browne Collection. She is also the president of the Sylvia Browne Corporation and the founder of her church, the Society of Novus Spiritus.

Chris Dufresne

Chris is the son of Sylvia Browne. Like his mother, Chris is a gifted and highly respected psychic in his own right who has been in practice for more than 20 years. He is the author of *Christmas in Heaven, Animals on the Other Side*, *My Life with Sylvia Browne,* and *My Psychic Journey*.
Sylvia and Chris both work in Campbell, California.

For more information about Sylvia Browne and Chris Dufresne, please visit their website www.sylvia.org.

Also from Sylvia Browne and Chris Dufresne

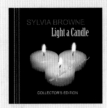

STRENGTH

Bless my home
with the presence
of animal spirits and
totems. Let the strength,
courage, and loyalty
of animals reflect
on me and allow my
spirit to reflect their
soul's perfection.
—Sylvia C. Browne

Visit our website to see the
Sylvia Browne Collection and
sign up to receive our monthly
e-coupons and special new
product announcements.

www.angelbea.com